WHO, WHA

WHO WERE

The Abolitionists?

DANIKA COOLEY

CF4·K

10 9 8 7 6 5 4 3 2 1
Copyright © Danika Cooley 2023
Paperback ISBN: 978-1-5271-1009-0
ebook ISBN: 978-1-5271-1077-9

Published by
Christian Focus Publications,
Geanies House, Fearn, Tain, Ross-shire,
IV20 1TW, Scotland, U.K.
www.christianfocus.com
email: info@christianfocus.com

Printed and bound by Bell and Bain, Glasgow

Cover design by Catriona Mackenzie
Illustrations by Martyn Smith

TABLE OF CONTENTS

Dedication

To every History Detective. May you use your gifts for God's glory in all you do.

THE AUTHOR

Danika Cooley and her husband, Ed, are committed to leading their children to life for the glory of God. Danika has a passion for equipping parents to teach the Bible and Christian history to their kids. She is the author of *Help Your Kids Learn and Love the Bible, When Lightning Struck!: The Story of Martin Luther, Wonderfully Made: God's Story of Life from Conception to Birth*, and the *Who, What, Why?* Series about the history of our faith. Danika's three year Bible survey curriculum, Bible Road Trip™, is used by families around the world. Weekly, she encourages tens of thousands of parents to intentionally raise biblically literate children. Danika is a homeschool mother of four with a bachelor of arts degree from the University of Washington. Find her at ThinkingKidsBlog.org.

FOR SUCH A
TIME AS THIS

Courageous people do not usually intend to be brave. Instead, God's people use the gifts he gives them to glorify God and to serve others. As we look back upon the lives of people in the past, we see how God orchestrates every event to help his children grow in character and to accomplish a specific role in his story of the world. Some lives seem unusually difficult, and some people come to faith in Jesus after terrible sin. It is always fascinating to see how God's people impact history.

Do you know the story of Esther in the Bible? She was a Jewish girl who married Ahasuerus, the king of Persia. Now Ahasuerus was a real hothead. He sent his first wife away just because he was angry. Ahasuerus' anger was so legendary that people in history told stories about it. One story, which is not in the Bible, says that while Ahasuerus was on his way to attack Greece, he ordered his men to build a rope bridge across a strait. The ropes were broken to pieces by rough water during a storm. Ahasuerus was so furious that he had his men whip the water three hundred times. That was the kind of man young Esther was made to marry. You might imagine she was nervous about her new husband. You may just be right.

Now, after Esther and Ahasuerus married, an evil counselor to Ahasuerus named Haman plotted to destroy the Jews. Because Esther and her uncle Mordecai were Jews, Mordecai instructed Esther to approach her husband and ask him to save the Jews. Esther explained that she very well might die for the impertinent act of initiating a visit to the throne room.

Wise Mordecai replied, "Do not think to yourself that in the king's palace you will escape any more than all the other Jews.

For if you keep silent at this time, relief and deliverance will rise for the Jews from another place, but you and your father's house will perish."

Looking back on the events of Esther's life, Mordecai's advice to Esther makes a lot of sense, doesn't it? Esther was, indeed, placed in a specific

time and place for "such a time as this." Even though she was married to a hot-headed king and even though she had to risk her life, Esther was in a position to help her people.

The Bible tells us that God is sovereign over all of history. That means he is the ruler of time, events, kings, and ordinary people. During the time of global slavery, when God's created human beings were owned like cattle across the world, men and women who loved Jesus fasted, prayed, and—like Esther—refused to be silent in the face of injustice.

From AD 1688 until 1888, thousands of abolitionists joined the fight to end slavery. Most abolitionists—

people who fought to abolish, or end, the slave trade—were motivated by their love for Jesus and for God's Word. They spoke, wrote, and preached about God's love for all people. Often, they risked their lives to love their neighbors as themselves in the fight to end slavery. Sometimes they even broke man's law to honor God's law.

We are going to take a look at the lives of ten abolitionists who dedicated their lives to glorifying God. They were black and white, poor and rich, enslaved and free. Many Christian abolitionists knew each other and sometimes they worked together to help free human souls. Each one used the gifts God gave them to serve him in the best way they were able. In the end, we know that God in his providence—that means the way God cares for us and arranges the events of our lives—planned the lives of the abolitionists "for such a time as this."

THE SIN AFTER THE SIN

As Europeans began sailing the world and taking over other countries, many people—especially Africans—were enslaved. Slave owners wanted free labor for plantations or farms, which grew crops like cotton,

Zachary Macauley   William Knibb   Sojourner Truth

coffee, or sugar. Chattel slavery—treating people like property—was a terrible sin.

Every sin has a way of producing more sin. Many slaves were kept from reading God's Word, praying, or learning about Jesus. Slavery also destroyed families. After all, when people are treated like cattle, marriage

Harriet Tubman

Frederick Douglass

13

and children are not cared for. God created us to worship him and live in families, and the sin of slavery hurt the hearts of the abolitionists, just as it must hurt our hearts.

Granville Sharp

Phillis Wheatley

GRANVILLE SHARP
(1735-1813)

Granville Sharp was a pastor's son. Out of fourteen children, only six—Granville and five older brothers—survived into adulthood. During a time without antibiotics or other life-saving medications, childhood death was pretty normal. Like most lower- and middle-

Olaudah Equiano

Thomas Clarkson

William Wilberforce

class teen boys in England in the mid-1750s, Granville left home to earn a living at the age of fifteen.

Granville loved theology—the study of God and his Word—so he used his spare time to learn Greek and Hebrew. By the age of twenty-three, he was working for the British Government as a clerk. By the age of thirty, Granville was also publishing about the Bible nearly every year.

If you ever read God's Word in the original Greek language, you will certainly use "Sharp's Rule." The rule showed that the authors of the New Testament called Jesus both God and Savior. Jesus is the second person of the Trinity—the one, true God in whom there are three persons, Father, Son, and Holy Spirit. Knowing that Jesus is God the Son and the Son of God is a very important thing to know.

Now, if that rule about how to read Greek was all that Granville Sharp left behind in this world, he would

have done something very important with his life. In fact, that was just a small part of his work in God's big universe. In 1765, the same year Granville published his first theological work, he visited his brother, William. William was living his own "for such a time as this" life, working as a free doctor for the very poor in London.

In William's waiting room, Granville met Jonathan Strong. Jonathan had been horribly beaten by his slave owner with the handle of a gun, then left to die in the streets of London.

Sin leads to more sin. Slavery stole God's Word from people who were enslaved. It stole God's good gift of family and marriage from millions. Slavery also rotted the souls of the enslavers. They became murderers and thieves, taking what was not theirs, and killing enslaved humans with no consequences here on this earth.

Jonathan survived his owner's attempt to kill him, then Granville and William cared for his wounds for two years. When he finally looked healthy, Jonathan's owner—the man who beat him—tried to kidnap and sell him. So, Granville threatened to sue the owner, who left Jonathan alone. Jonathan finally died of his wounds. He died free, but still murdered.

Jonathan's life and suffering showed Granville God's calling on his life. He would write about the Bible, he would study the law, and he would sue kidnappers. Then he would sue them some more. Granville was not a lawyer, but he was involved in each case. This crusade cost him every penny he had, and his brothers ended up supporting him. Granville never married. He was too busy suing all the slave owners.

Granville knew that if the court system decided in favor of an enslaved human soul—that's what Jesus called slaves in Revelation 18:13, human souls—then it would set a precedent. A precedent is a legal decision that affects all following legal decisions. Precedents are incredibly important.

After helping in lawsuits for five more kidnapped slaves, Granville helped James Somerset. James was a slave in Massachusetts—a British colony in America at the time. He was brought to England where he escaped and then was kidnapped to be sold in Jamaica. In the English court case of the century, with Granville's help, James was freed. Kidnapping people from England to sell elsewhere was outlawed. This was the first major event in a long history of events that helped end

slavery in England and across the world. Everyone knew about the James Somerset case.

Now, Granville didn't win every case, but that did not stop him. In 1774, Olaudah Equiano, a Nigerian who eventually purchased his own freedom, asked Granville for help in the case of a kidnapped friend. Granville lost the case and Olaudah's friend was killed in slavery. Later, Olaudah brought Granville another injustice—the Zong case. This time, one hundred and thirty-four kidnapped Africans had been thrown off a slave ship on the way to the Americas. Olaudah wanted justice for their murder. The slave ship owners filed an insurance claim for lost property. Granville argued that not only should they receive no money, but they should also be tried for murder. In the end, no one was charged in the mass death of the Africans. It was a terrible injustice.

Granville died in his late seventies, about twenty years before all British slaves were freed. During his life, he saw slaves in England freed and he witnessed the end of the British slave trade. Granville was friends with abolitionists across the world. He loved Jesus and he spent his life writing about his Savior and fighting for God's people.

PHILLIS WHEATLEY
(c. 1753-1784)

Four years before Granville met Jonathan Sharp in England, a little girl stood on an auction block in Boston, wrapped in a dirty piece of carpet, missing her front baby teeth. Susanna Wheatley bought her to be a maid and named her after the slaving ship, Phillis, on which she arrived from Africa.

God is the King of all of history. He ordains—arranges—every event. God is the sovereign King of the Universe—the ruler of everything. In Acts 17:26-27a, Luke writes: "And he made from one man every nation of mankind to live on all the face of the earth, having determined allotted periods and the boundaries of their dwelling place, that they should

seek God, and perhaps feel their way toward him and find him." God made all people from one man—Adam. All ethnicities are from God, and all are part of the same family. God also made the boundaries of nations and periods of time. All of this is to point people to salvation in Jesus.

Phillis lived during the Age of Enlightenment, a time when philosophers—men who debate big ideas—were busy trying to find truth while ignoring the Bible. Naturally, a lot of their ideas were wrong because all truth comes from God. Around the year Phillis was born, a philosopher wrote that Africans were not really human. Three years after Phillis was shipped to America, another philosopher said he didn't think Africans could be artists or scientists because none of the slaves he had seen—who were busy surviving—seemed creative.

Phillis would one day answer the philosophers. But first, she had to learn English. Susanna and John Wheatley's teen daughter, Mary, taught Phillis to read. Not only did Phillis quickly learn a second language—English, and a third—Latin, she read the Bible and taught herself to write. Phillis loved Jesus. We can assume she met him in the pages of Scripture. When she was thirteen years old, her first poem was published in a newspaper, submitted by Susanna.

Phillis was sixteen when the Boston Massacre—a riot started by American rebels and ended by English soldiers with guns—happened just down the street from the Wheatley house. Phillis wrote a poem about "freedom's cause." The same year, Phillis wrote a poem about the death of George Whitefield— the English evangelist who preached over eighteen thousand times to more than ten million people during the First Great Awakening. Phillis' poem about Whitefield was printed and sold in America and London as a poster just after he died.

Then, Susanna tried to raise money to print a book of twenty-eight of Phillis' poems. But, even though Phillis' poetry was very popular, no one believed she wrote it. The philosophers who wrote that Africans could not create art were winning people over with their strange, unbiblical logic.

Phillis was not the kind of abolitionist who spoke to large crowds about the Bible and freedom. Rather, Phillis found herself proving to the world that she was, in fact, a person. To prove her humanity, Phillis had a trial of sorts in front of eighteen of the most well-known men in the American colonies. Pastors, the governor of Massachusetts, writers, scholars, and politicians questioned Phillis until they were convinced she wrote her poems, then they signed a letter promising she was the author.

Phillis' poetry book was finally published in England in 1773, just two years before the American

Revolution, when the American colonies fought the British for freedom. The Wheatleys finally freed Phillis a month after the publication of her book, at the age of twenty, when English people questioned why she was still in bondage.

The United States of America came into being with the signing of the Declaration of Independence on the 4th of July, 1776. Phillis met and impressed three important American founders—John Hancock, who signed the Declaration of Independence, future president George Washington, and Benjamin Franklin. Sadly, the main author of the Declaration of Independence, Thomas Jefferson, dismissed Phillis' intelligence and talent, saying that no black person could possibly create true art.

Phillis Wheatley's poetry—written while she was an enslaved teen—was brilliant. Phillis expresses gratitude for her saving faith in Jesus. She speaks of being torn from her parents and the pain that caused. In a letter to a Native American pastor, Phillis wrote that God has implanted a love of freedom in humans and he grants deliverance in his own way. Then, she criticizes white Americans for crying for freedom for themselves as they abused power over African and Native Americans.

Phillis Wheatley married grocer John Peters and had three children who all died very young. She died at just thirty-one years old. Phillis started the great tradition of African American literature. More importantly, she used her God-given talents to remind the world she was, indeed, a child of God—human.

OLAUDAH EQUIANO
(c.1745-1797)

While Phillis Wheatley was proving that Africans were human, Olaudah Equiano was busy making the history he would one day write about. Olaudah once said that if he were a European, he would call his sufferings great. Instead, he looked back on the events of his life and saw how even the worst events pointed to God's providence—his care for Olaudah.

Olaudah's father was a tribal elder in Nigeria where the people loved dancing and dyed their clothes bright blue. The youngest of seven living children, Olaudah adored his mother. When Olaudah was just eleven years old, he and his sister were kidnapped by African slave traders while their parents worked in the fields. Olaudah was separated from his sister and sold westward across Africa from tribe to tribe. Eventually, Olaudah was sold to white men and put on a ship to Virginia. On the trip, he saw many people die. Olaudah's written account of the Middle Passage—the trip from Africa to the Americas—would one day help people to understand the horrors of the slave trade.

Olaudah lived a fascinating life. Though Olaudah spent some time on land, he sailed much of his life and was even drafted into the British Navy during the Seven Years War. He traveled to the states of Virginia, Pennsylvania, South Carolina, and Georgia in America, and to many places throughout Britain and Scotland—including London, a place he loved.

There's more. Olaudah sailed to islands of the West Indies like the Bahamas, Montserrat, St. Kitts, Barbados, and Grenada. He visited France and the islands off its coast. Olaudah saw the coastal areas of Italy, Turkey, Portugal, Spain, and Costa Rica. He even traveled on an Arctic expedition north of Norway and stayed for a while on the coast of what is now Nicaragua and Honduras.

As he traveled, Olaudah saw amazing things. There were roaring beasts in African forests, flying fish, giant whales, and a large shark dragged on board his ship. In America, he shot alligators trying to climb into his boat and mistook flamingos for large men. Olaudah saw huge caravans with hundreds of camels from India. Once, his ship was attacked by a herd of seahorses. That sounds strange, but big-belly seahorses can grow up to thirty-five centimeters in length. That's nearly fourteen inches—about the size of a chihuahua.

Olaudah was kidnapped and sold repeatedly. He learned several languages, went to war, was forced to fight other boys, and was robbed multiple times. Olaudah lived through smallpox, explosions, fires, shipwrecks, and an attack that hospitalized him. Once, he fell from the top deck of a ship far down into the hold below.

The entire time, Olaudah was looking for God. Olaudah would see men reading the Bible. When no one was looking, he would speak to a Bible and then hold it to his ear to see if it replied. It never did. So, Olaudah learned to read. He visited churches on land and once saw a church in Georgia with ladders up

against the windows. People were leaning in to hear George Whitefield preach. Olaudah, who was around twenty-three, had never seen a man so passionate about Jesus.

A year later, Olaudah purchased his own freedom by buying items in one place and selling them for more money in another. That's when he met an old sailor who took him to a church where he heard the gospel. Olaudah learned he couldn't be saved by his good works. Just one sin would keep him from God's love. But Jesus paid the price of sin for all who believe in him, confess him as Lord, and follow him with their lives. Jesus made a way for sinners to be adopted by God the Father as his very own children. Olaudah was saved through Jesus' sacrifice for him. Olaudah read the Bible, prayed, and came to know the God he had looked for his whole life.

Now free, Olaudah—as a part of a group called the Sons of Africa—wrote letters in favor of abolition to newspapers. He even sent a petition to Queen Charlotte of England asking her to free Africans from slavery. In 1788, the same year the British Parliament announced an investigation into the slave trade, Olaudah published his story, *The Interesting Narrative of the Life of Olaudah Equiano.*

This made Olaudah a best-selling author who traveled through the British Empire, talking about Africa, slavery, freedom, and how he came to serve Jesus. His book was translated into Dutch, German, French, and Russian. On his book tour, Olaudah married a lady named Susannah and together they had two little girls. Susannah died four years into their marriage. A little over a year later, Olaudah also died.

Olaudah's book about his life changed the way people saw slavery. Readers everywhere paid attention when Olaudah asked Christians how they could follow Jesus yet support enslaving Africans. After all, Jesus taught, "as you wish that others would do to you, do so to them" (Luke 6:31).

THOMAS CLARKSON (1760-1846)

After Granville Sharp argued on behalf of people enslaved in England, after Phillis Wheatley's brilliant poems proved she was a person, and nine years before Olaudah Equiano published his book about being kidnapped as an African boy, Thomas, the youngest of three children of a pastor and school headmaster, entered an essay contest at Cambridge University. It was 1785 and the essay contest question was "Is it lawful to make slaves of others against their will?"

Exodus 21:16 says that enslaving and selling people is a crime worthy of death, but Thomas wanted to share even more evidence against slavery. Thomas loved to discover facts. First, Thomas read a book by American Quaker Anthony Benezet which described different people groups in northern and western Africa. Then, Thomas interviewed students who had personally seen or been involved with slavery in some way. He read his finished essay aloud to the judges and won the contest.

That could have been the end of Thomas' story as we know it, but God had other plans. On his way home to London, Thomas was so upset about what he'd learned about slavery that he sat down on the ground beside his horse to think. Thomas hadn't been guilty of the sin of slavery, but he was guilty of other sins. Thomas decided he would follow Jesus his whole life—and that his whole life would be dedicated to ending slavery.

Thomas translated his essay from Latin into English so he could spread it far and wide across the country. That's when Thomas met Granville Sharp and they formed a committee to abolish the slave trade. The committee needed information to help people in the British government understand that slavery was evil. Thomas was, of course, in charge of research.

Thomas and Granville also needed at least one member of Parliament to help end the slave trade. In 1787, Thomas gave William Wilberforce a copy of his essay and asked him to join the fight against slavery. Seven months later, William committed to help. He, too, would spend his whole life fighting slavery. He just needed Thomas to bring him facts—lots and lots of facts.

The next year, Thomas traveled across the country. In just two months, he rode his horse sixteen hundred miles. He interviewed twenty thousand sailors. Now, we know that sin creates more sin. Many of the sailors on slave trading ships were treated terribly. Some had been kidnapped themselves. Sometimes, they were even murdered like the slaves on the ships. It was just more sin. Thomas was horrified by all of it.

As he traveled, Thomas spoke to crowds of regular English people, showing the shackles and thumb screws sailors used to restrain enslaved Africans. He handed out a diagram of Africans packed tightly side by side in the bottom of a ship. Along his route, Thomas helped people form abolition societies, leaving

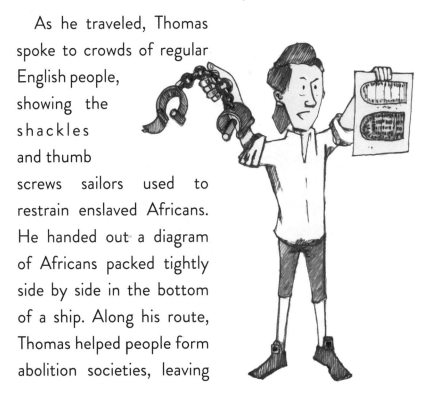

pamphlets and pictures for new abolitionists to share with neighbors and friends. It wasn't easy. Thomas was mugged and threatened by people who loved slavery and hated the one true God.

Thomas kept working. He wrote a number of books and pamphlets, hoping to convince the British people to protest against enslavement. In 1789, he traveled to Paris, hoping to co
as well. Then he tra
again, researching
used his research
the slave trade.

After seven years of long and stressful research trips, Thomas' health was in danger. He took a long rest from his research work and married a lady named Catherine. Together they had one little boy, Thomas.

In 1806, Thomas hit the road once more, asking audiences to urge members of Parliament to vote against the slave trade. The very next year, Britain ended the selling of humans. While Britain didn't free those who were already enslaved, not enslaving additional Africans was cause for celebration. Thomas wrote a book on the history of the abolition of the slave trade in Britain.

Thomas had committed to help end slavery—it was God's calling on his life. The work wasn't finished, so he, William, and Granville formed the Society of the Abolition of the Slave Trade. They worked another ten years to free slaves in all the British territories.

Next, Thomas worked to end slavery in countries like the United States and Brazil. In 1840, Thomas spoke to thousands of delegates at the first World Antislavery Convention in London. The convention looked at slavery in America, India, Africa, the Middle East, Asia, and Latin America. There was still much more work to be done.

Thomas died nearly two decades before slaves in the United States were freed by a massive war. He used his gifts—and his life—to glorify God by fighting for an end to the enslavement of God's created image bearers.

WILLIAM WILBERFORCE (1759-1833)

Born the year before Thomas Clarkson, William Wilberforce had every advantage in life until his father died when he was just nine years old. Still, William's family was quite wealthy, which meant William was rich—and very, very spoiled. William's aunt and uncle lived near his boarding school and introduced him to the teachings of pastors like John Newton, John Wesley, and George Whitefield.

William was excited about the ideas of evangelicals— Christians who believed that the good news of Jesus should be preached above all else and that good works should follow salvation. Now, William's mother, Elizabeth, preferred the traditions of the Church of England. So, she moved her son away from his family and put him in a different boarding school.

William was easily distracted. He went to parties, played cards, and often did nothing at all. For fun, and maybe out of boredom, William ran for Parliament

and won in 1780 when he was just twenty-one years old. William was still without God, so still he went to parties, played cards, and often did nothing at all. The only difference was that he made speeches— extraordinarily good speeches, as it turns out.

Sometimes, instead of doing nothing at all, William traveled during his vacations. When he was twenty-five, he went to the French Riviera with his mother, sister, and friend Isaac. Isaac spent the entire trip speaking to William about the good news of Jesus. Together they read a book on Jesus. After one more trip with Isaac, William believed in Jesus, repented of—or turned from—his sins, and was saved.

Right away, William's life was different. He abandoned his lazy lifestyle and committed to helping people in need. He also decided to give away at least one quarter of his income every year.

William was so worried he was wasting his life that he decided to visit one of those evangelical preachers he had heard of as a child, John Newton. John's mother died when he was just seven, so he became a sailor like his father, eventually working in the slave trade—even for several years after Jesus saved him. Sometimes, people are convicted of their sins slowly, over time. That was the case for John.

At the end of 1785 when he met with William, John was a pastor with the Church of England. He deeply regretted his part in selling human souls. Two years later, God used his evil experience for good when his pamphlet on the abuses of the slave industry would be read in Parliament. John told William that God probably raised William into public service to do his will for the good of the nation—for such a time as this.

About a year later, Thomas Clarkson asked William to join the fight for abolition in England. In 1789, the same year Olaudah Equiano's book was published, and the same year a young man named Zachary Macaulay sailed home from Jamaica, the year after a famous poet named Hannah More wrote a poem

called "Slavery," William Wilberforce stood in front of the British Parliament and gave his first speech against the slave trade. William fought for an end to slavery and for the freedom of all slaves in the British Empire for more than forty-five years. Can you imagine persevering in a fight against one evil for that long?

Thomas, William, Zachary, Hannah, Granville Sharp, Thomas Babington, William's brother-in-law lawyer James Stephen, and banker Henry Thornton formed a Christian group of friends known as the Clapham Sect. They were evangelicals belonging to the Church of England, committed to the end of slavery in Britain. William was especially good friends with poet Hannah More who quietly campaigned for abolition amongst the wealthier women in Britain, organizing a sugar boycott. Women in England stopped buying sugar—a sugar boycott—because it was grown using slave labor. William married a Christian lady named Barbara and they had six children.

Over and over, William spoke, introduced new legislation, and presented petitions with hundreds of thousands of signatures. Over and over, Parliament voted against ending slavery. William even wrote a three-hundred-and-fifty-page book against the slave trade. Preacher John Wesley once wrote William to encourage him, saying that if God raised him up to fight slavery, no one could really be against him.

Finally, nearly two decades later in 1807, William's colleagues voted to end the selling of human souls. William wept. Then, he kept working for the freedom of all slaves throughout the British Empire for another twenty-six years. Just three days before he died, the captives were freed.

After his salvation, William did the exact opposite of nothing at all. He worked to see slavery ended. He promoted missions and a Bible society. William fought against dangerous child labor, and made sure the poor had food and prisoners were cared for. More than anything, William cared about people hearing the good news of Jesus.

ZACHARY MACAULAY
(1768-1838)

Born two years after Olaudah purchased his own freedom, Zachary Macaulay loved numbers. Even though he was born blind in one eye, the Scottish minister's son taught himself to read Greek, Latin, and French. Zachary had a lot of time to study. You see, at the age of nine Zachary badly broke his arm. Doctors in the 1700s didn't have medication to help people sleep through surgery, so Zachary had surgery—twice—while he was awake. It took five years for his arm to heal.

As soon as Zachary could use his arm, his father sent fourteen-year-old Zachary to the big city to count money for a merchant. That's when things started to go awry—that means off the course one has planned. First, Zachary had planned to go to college. Second, Zachary's father had planned for him to be a Christian. After all, he was a minister and he had told Zachary the good news of Jesus.

Instead, Zachary went to the big city and heard the teachings of the philosophers—the exact same men who wrote that black people weren't human. These philosophers said other wicked things—that the Bible wasn't true and God wasn't real. Zachary not only believed these terrible things, he tried to convince others the lies were true as well.

Sin always leads to more sin, and sin is always discovered. Zachary got himself into so much trouble that at sixteen he had to leave the country aboard a slave ship to work on a Jamaican plantation. At first, the violence and humiliation poured out on enslaved Africans hurt his heart. Over time, though, as Zachary whipped slaves, he stopped caring about their pain.

In his letter to Timothy, Paul says some people will follow false teachers, who are liars "whose consciences

are seared" (1 Timothy 4:2). When healthy skin is burned with hot metal, the skin eventually scars and scar tissue lacks sensitivity.

Your conscience—the feeling God gives you to know right from wrong—can become seared—burnt and then scarred—if you believe false teachers, or if you sin repeatedly. Now, Zachary had believed false teachers and he had sinned over and over. His conscience was badly seared. He was guilty of sin, but he couldn't feel his guilt.

Zachary returned to England in 1789—the same year Olaudah Equiano published his narrative. He went to live with his sister, Jean, and her husband, Thomas Babington. Thomas was a rich young man who loved Jesus and used his money to help those in need. Through Thomas, twenty-one-year-old Zachary came to know Jesus. The Bible tells us that when we are saved, God replaces our heart of stone with a heart of flesh. That's a great word picture, isn't it? Now that Zachary loved Jesus, his conscience was no longer seared.

Zachary joined the Clapham Sect. Thomas and Jean, Granville, Thomas Clarkson, William, Hannah More, and others were working together to end slavery, each using their God-given gift. Zachary's gifting was the ability to read numbers and understand their significance. He would read massive reports about slavery, then sit in the gallery of Parliament to give William Wilberforce just the right facts at just the right time during William's speeches.

From 1791 to 1799, twenty-two-year-old Zachary became part of an experiment to help freed blacks settle in Africa in a colony called Sierra Leone. As the governor, Zachary ran the colony and helped protect settlers against kidnappers. He also taught both children and adults to read the Bible. The colony faced massive challenges. Lots of people died of germs—colonists, missionaries, and people sent to help run the colony. Ships full of pirates attacked. The Sierra Leone experiment didn't help former slaves the way Christian abolitionists hoped it would.

In the middle of his time in Sierra Leone, Zachary was so sick with malaria that he sailed home on a slave ship, sleeping in the hull with the captives. Zachary took careful notes on the conditions aboard the ship. He stayed in Barbados long enough to write reports on every aspect of how enslaved people lived.

Once he moved back to England in 1799, Zachary

testified before Parliament. Two years after the formation of the Anti-Slavery Society in 1823, the Clapham Sect made Zachary the writer and editor for a new newspaper, the Anti-Slavery Reporter. Zachary spent the next five years explaining hard-to-understand things to readers. Once, Zachary read more than seven hundred pages about slavery in the English territories, then wrote a twenty-three-page article explaining what all the numbers meant.

Zachary married a Christian teacher named Selina Mills and they had nine children together. He frequently thanked God for the blessings in his life. Zachary died five years after all British slaves were freed. Though he started his life hating God, he spent many years loving and serving Jesus.

WILLIAM KNIBB
(1803-1845)

William Knibb was born in England, one of eight children, four years after Zachary Macaulay testified before Parliament and just three years before Thomas Clarkson set off on his second trip to collect more evidence against the slave trade. By the time William was four years old, the slave trade was abolished in

both Britain and America, but that did not free the people who were already enslaved.

Now, William loved his older brother Thomas, so he followed him everywhere. First, William followed Thomas to school, then to Sunday School when he was seven. Next, William followed Thomas to work as a printer. William was only thirteen years old, but that is

how growing up worked in those days. When Thomas was baptized as a Christian, so was William. In 1822, Thomas went to teach reading, writing, and the good news of Jesus at a school for freed blacks in Jamaica for the Baptist Missionary Society. Sadly, Thomas died a year after arriving in Jamaica. In 1824, William followed Thomas one last time, bringing his new wife, Mary, to the island of Jamaica.

The Baptist missionaries instructed William to talk only about Jesus, not about slavery. Right away, William hated slavery. He called it a monster, a child of hell, compared it to a disease, and said it killed morality. The beatings enslaved people received appalled William.

William set about building a new school in Kingston and began teaching two hundred children six days each week. He preached and taught Sunday School to more than five hundred people on the seventh day. To show the work his students were doing—and how very smart and human they were—William sent schoolwork samples to England, which people nicknamed the "Slave Book."

Frustrated by slavery, a deacon at William's church organized a work strike just after Christmas in 1831. No one was supposed to get hurt, but the strike quickly became an insurrection. This "Baptist War" lasted for two months and involved almost sixty thousand enslaved people. Plantations were burnt to the ground and fourteen white people were killed. Angry plantation owners retaliated, killing five hundred slaves, attacking missionaries, and burning down churches and Christian schoolrooms, including William's church. William convinced his congregation not to riot, but he was still arrested and thrown in jail for nearly two months. Missionaries fled while William's family went into hiding. Fifty plantation owners stoned his home while William hid on a ship.

William took his family—he and Mary had ten children—and sailed for England. As William spoke to the Baptist Missionary Society, the secretary tugged on the tails of William's coat to tell him to sit down and be quiet. Instead, William asked God to open the eyes of Christians in England to the evil of slavery. He called on English families to listen to his descriptions of terrible abuse from plantation owners. William refused to be quiet.

In fact, William toured England, Scotland, and Ireland, speaking about the suffering of his African brothers and sisters. He traveled over six thousand miles in five months, telling Christians they must help their enslaved brothers and sisters. He spoke to over two hundred thousand people at one hundred and fifty-four meetings. Still, William refused to be quiet. He spoke for days in front of special committees for both houses of Parliament.

In the end, no one could silence William—not the plantation owners, not the military, not the missionary secretary. William spoke until Britain finally passed the Slavery Abolition Act in 1833. The Act instituted a six-year apprenticeship system that was a form of half-way slavery, so William kept talking, inspiring an early end to apprenticeship. William was so excited slavery was over, at midnight on July 31st in 1838, he rang the bell of his church in Jamaica, yelling, "The monster is dead!" He threw a pair of shackles in a coffin and buried it under a tombstone that read: "Colonial Slavery. Died July 31, 1838. Age 276 years."

William didn't end his life work with the end of enslavement. Instead, he rebuilt Jamaican churches and schools with money from English abolitionists. Then, he translated the Bible into the Jamaican language of Creole and taught freed blacks to read God's Word. With the help of around twenty Baptist missionaries, William saw twenty-two thousand new Christians follow Jesus and be baptized during a seven-year revival called the Jamaica Awakening. William personally baptized thousands of new Christians. William even convinced the Baptist Missionary Society to begin sharing the good news of Jesus in Africa.

Then, William raised money and purchased thousands of acres of land where blacks could build their own homes in villages. William helped found thirty-five churches, twenty-four missions, and sixteen schools. When William died of a tropical fever, at age forty-two, eight thousand Jamaicans attended his funeral. Mary stayed in Jamaica another twenty-five years with the people she and William loved.

SOJOURNER TRUTH
(1797-1883)

You probably know how many brothers and sisters you have. Sojourner Truth did not know whether she had nine siblings or eleven. She was born around the same year Olaudah Equiano died, maybe five years before the birth of William Knibb. Like most slaves, Sojourner did not know the date—or even the year—of her birth.

The man who owned Sojourner's family ran a hotel in New York state. He sold Sojourner's brothers and sisters as soon as they were toddlers. Sojourner's mother missed her children terribly. She would point at the moon and tell Sojourner, "Your brothers and sisters are under this same moon. They can see God's work, too." Sojourner prayed often, out loud, and God always answered her prayers. She didn't know that God could hear silent prayers, nor did she know that Jesus—God the Son and the Son of God—died to pay the price for the sins of his followers. Sojourner didn't know Jesus loved her at all.

At age nine, Sojourner was sold at an auction for one hundred dollars. The people who bought her were cruel, so Sojourner prayed for a new family. God answered her prayer, and she went to live on a large farm. About a year and a half later, she was sold again to a man who kept her for eighteen years.

Sojourner was forced to marry a much older slave and had five children. After Sojourner's owner lied about freeing her, she took her baby and left her enslavement, finding employment with a couple who paid the ransom for Sojourner and her baby to be free. Remember, one of the sins that grows from the sin of slavery is the destruction of families. God gives us families as one of his good gifts. Sojourner lost years with her parents and children.

Sojourner's story is full of answered prayers. At one point, her five-year-old son was illegally sold out of state into the Deep South where the plantation life was brutal. Sojourner walked, barefooted, into the courts run by white men and told her story over and over again. Of course, she prayed to God the entire time. Though little Peter was covered in deep scars, Sojourner recovered him—all the while receiving exactly the help she prayed for. She was the first black woman to win a court case of that kind against a white man.

Now, remember that slavery also robbed people of

knowing God and the Bible. Sojourner could not read or write and was deprived of God's Word. Eventually, Sojourner heard the good news of Jesus and was saved. Suddenly, she realized she had been very demanding— and not at all respectful—of the Lord of the Universe in her prayers. She exclaimed out loud, "Oh, God, I did not know you were so big!" Sojourner was sometimes confused about God's will for us and briefly joined a cult—a false religion that almost seems right but is not biblical.

As a free woman, Sojourner worked in New York City, taught about Jesus' love, and set up prayer meetings as people were saved in Jesus through the good news of the gospel. Sojourner went places no one else would and shared the love of Jesus with ladies no one else wanted to talk to.

Then, one day, Sojourner decided she needed to help even more people. New York just wasn't big enough for everything she had to share with others. So, she put some clothes in a pillowcase, twenty-five cents in her pocket, and a little food in a basket. For

a long time, Sojourner walked across the northern United States, staying in the homes of strangers at night. She met many Christians and shared the gospel everywhere she went. Sojourner spoke often to large crowds about slavery and freedom, and about treating women and black people well. Sojourner also spoke alongside abolitionists like William Lloyd Garrison and Frederick Douglass.

In 1850, Sojourner published the story of her life. Because she couldn't write, her friend Olive Gilbert wrote the story down for

her. Sojourner's story left out much of the abuse she endured but is full of answered prayers. More than anything, it showed the sins that grew out of the sin of slavery. Enslaved people were robbed of family, of knowing God through his Word, and of dignity and freedom.

During the American Civil War, when the North fought the South to end slavery, Sojourner continued to serve others, working in the refugee camps of Washington

DC, where now freed southern slaves gathered in throngs as the United States decided how to help them. Sojourner even visited President Abraham Lincoln.

When Sojourner died around the age of eighty-six, she had spoken to thousands and met the president. Through her faithful service and witness, many learned to hate slavery and respect women. Much more importantly, many people learned of the love of Jesus for his children.

FREDERICK DOUGLASS (c.1817-1895)

Frederick Douglass was born on a plantation in Maryland, ten years after both America and Britain ended their slave trade. Still, slavery was allowed to continue as long as new slaves were not brought from Africa. Frederick was raised by his grandmother until the age of seven, along with his three siblings. Frederick only met his mother a few times in the middle of the night, when she sneaked in to see him. Frederick was robbed of God's good gift of family.

Frederick wore only a knee-length shirt year-round. Once a day, he ate corn meal poured into a trough. Frederick was always hungry and always cold. At seven, he was sent to Baltimore to be a caregiver to a boy, Thomas, who was even younger than he was. At first, the boy's mother was kind and gentle. Owning a person changed her, though, and she became angry and cruel. Frederick rebelled against her rules, secretly teaching himself to read by the age of twelve. Increasingly, he grew to hate being enslaved.

At the age of twenty-one, after years of brutal beatings and being passed to different members of his original

owner's family, Frederick escaped to the North. In New York, he met Underground Railroad conductor David Ruggles. The Underground Railroad was a secret network of blacks and whites in America who helped fugitive slaves escape from enslavement. David took Frederick to an underground station—a safe place to spend the night—and helped Frederick marry a free woman from Baltimore, Anna. Then, David sent them to Massachusetts.

In 1841 Frederick attended an abolitionist convention and told his story of slavery and escape. Frederick had scars on his back, but enslavers had

seared their consciences against God. After Frederick spoke, William Lloyd Garrison took the stage. Now, William was America's most famous abolitionist. William was also a Unitarian. Unitarians do not believe in salvation in Jesus, nor do they believe Jesus is God. William stood on the stage and asked the more than five hundred people in the audience if they had just heard the voice of a thing—or a man? "A man!" they all shouted.

That was the day that Frederick Douglass became an abolitionist. He traveled the northern United States speaking against slavery hundreds of times, often with William. In Indiana, Frederick was attacked by a pro-slavery mob. Once, he was dragged off a train. During those first years of speaking, Frederick was hit by rocks and rotten eggs, and his hand was broken.

In 1843, Frederick's book, *The Narrative of the Life of Frederick Douglass*, became an instant best-seller. Frederick used the names of all his oppressors in his story, exposing their sin. Many of the men and women who hurt him claimed to be Christians, preaching and leading Bible studies. Frederick himself was a Christian who loved Jesus, but he wanted people to see the difference between Christians who love their neighbors and people who twist God's Word for their own purposes.

Two years later, Frederick—who was still a fugitive—sailed for England where he spoke about American slavery. English abolitionists raised the money to ransom Frederick's freedom so he could return to America. They also raised money for him to begin his own abolitionist newspaper. Once home in 1847, Frederick and William started out on a lecture tour. William became terribly ill, so Frederick went on alone. In the basement of the African Methodist Episcopal Zion Church in New York, he began publishing *North Star.*

Frederick believed that the Constitution and Declaration of Independence were written to allow for abolition one day. He believed people should vote for the best candidate to end slavery eventually, even if the candidate wasn't perfect. He supported Republican Abraham Lincoln for president in 1860, just before the beginning of the Civil War. Frederick's willingness to use politics to end slavery also ended his friendship with William Lloyd Garrison.

Frederick worked for a long time to see the end of slavery. In 1852, he gave a fiery speech to whites on the Fourth of July—America's Independence Day.

He asked the audience if they were mocking him by asking him to speak on that day, pointing out that the Fourth of July was theirs, not his. He did not have the same blessings as those who were born free and allowed citizenship. Frederick couldn't even vote.

Frederick Douglass lived long after the Civil War when all American slaves were freed. He fought for civil rights, eventually seeing black men and women freed as slavery ended, then be granted rights as citizens of the United States. He saw, too, men of all races receive the right to vote.

Frederick's wife Anna died in 1882. They had five children. He married a white teacher named Helen in 1884. The day of his funeral, tens of thousands of people lined the streets, paying tribute to the man who had fought for the freedom and dignity of God's image bearers.

HARRIET TUBMAN
(c.1820-1913)

You've learned about people who loved Jesus and used their gifts and abilities to write, calculate numbers, speak, or research to end slavery. Our last abolitionist couldn't write, read, or calculate, and she wasn't much of a speaker. Harriet was a doer. She fixed injustice, one person at a time.

Harriet was one of nine children born to

slaves in Maryland, just four years before William and Mary Knibb sailed for Jamaica as missionaries. Harriet saw three of her sisters sold into the brutal Deep South, where people rarely reached freedom. Harriet's mother taught her to love Jesus with all her heart. By following Jesus, Harriet was freed from her sins. Harriet loved the story of Moses and the Exodus. When Harriet heard the story, she decided God wanted his people to be free—from their sins and from slavery.

Beginning at five years old, Harriet was rented out to other families—like a piece of farm equipment—to care for children, check muskrat traps, or work in the field. Like most slaves, Harriet was whipped and subjected to

terrible conditions. At thirteen, Harriet was in a store when a slave overseer threw a two-pound weight at another slave. The weight hit Harriet, cracking her skull and causing her brain to swell. For the rest of her life, Harriet would suddenly fall into a deep sleep no matter what she was doing. She often had vivid dreams she felt were God's way of showing her what to do next.

In 1849, twenty-eight-year-old Harriet learned that she, too, would be sold South, so she ran for freedom. Harriet followed the North Star, traveled at night, and prayed for guidance. She arrived in the land of the free with no one to greet her. Harriet missed her family—including her husband, John—terribly. She returned for her husband and found him married to another woman. Harriet was devastated. She decided to rescue as many of her family members as she could, starting that very trip. But first, she rescued a bunch of enslaved people from a nearby farm, taking them all the way to Canada.

Now, the Underground Railroad had already been operating for several decades in the United States with abolitionists helping fleeing slaves to safety. Most of the time, fugitive slaves started their journey on their own, running toward the North and praying for help. Not many people served as conductors—guides who actually went into the South to help rescue enslaved

people. Harriet, though, had a whole family in the South she loved and cared about. She wanted them to be free, too. In fact, if she picked up a few extra people each trip, she was happy to take them along to safety.

So, Harriet rescued her sister and her children. She rescued her parents and cared for them the rest of their lives. She rescued brothers and their wives or fiancées. Harriet rescued seventeen family members in all. Harriet also took along anyone willing to make the life-or-death journey to the North, as long as they were committed to finishing the trip. If anyone wanted to turn back, she threatened them with a gun. After

all, everyone in the group could be killed if the deserter was caught. Harriet gave children medicine to make them sleep the entire trip. She was one tough lady.

Throughout thirteen trips South to run off about seventy people, Harriet prayed. Through swamps, and rivers, and forests, God answered her prayers. There were narrow misses and blatant daytime rescues, but never once did any of Harriet's railroad passengers get caught. When asked how she could be so courageous, Harriet would reply that it wasn't her courage that she relied upon. No, Harriet trusted the Lord. As long as God wanted to use her life, he would keep her safe. As soon as God was done, she was ready to go to heaven.

By 1860, it was clear that all non-violent abolition efforts had failed. Many thousands of people were fleeing the South. In return, southern states left the union of America altogether. Abraham Lincoln was elected president, shots were fired, and the bloody civil war in America began. During the war, tens of thousands of slaves crossed the battle lines to the Union—or northern—side to find freedom. Huge refugee camps formed where wounded, hungry, and poorly clothed people huddled.

Harriet served as a nurse and a spy for the Union Army. Once, on a mission with several gun boats traveling upriver, enslaved plantation workers spotted Harriet and her troops. "Lincoln's gun boats!" they yelled. Eight hundred people ran through the water, carrying babies, children wrapped around their necks. Everyone climbed aboard, throwing chickens, pigs, and children on deck.

After the war, Harriet married a Union Army veteran and they adopted a daughter. When her husband died, she opened the Harriet Tubman Home for the Aged to care for poor, elderly black people. In the last two years of her life, Harriet's church took over the home and cared for her.

THIS TIME IN HISTORY

God ordains the events of our lives, putting us in just the right time and place to serve him just as he wants us to. God also gives each of his children a gift through the Holy Spirit.

Each one of the abolitionists used their gift to glorify God and to serve others. Each time they served the Lord, it impacted history.

Have you repented of your sin and committed to live for Jesus? When you glorify God and love his people, only God knows how he will use your life for just such a time as this.

TIMELINE

1735

Granville Sharp is born in England.

1745

Olaudah Equiano may have been born in Nigeria.

1753

This may be the year Phillis Wheatley is born in Africa.

Equiano is kidnapped and sold in Virginia. He sails for England, beginning his many adventures as a sailor.

1759

William Wilberforce is born in England.

1760

Thomas Clarkson is born in England.

1761

Wheatley is sold in Boston.

1765

Sharp publishes his first theological text.

Sharp meets Jonathan Strong, becomes an abolitionist.

Equiano hears George Whitefield preach in Georgia.

1766

Equiano purchases his freedom. He continues sailing.

1768

Zachary Macaulay is born in Scotland.

1770

The Boston Massacre takes place down the street from Wheatley.

Preacher George Whitefield dies. Wheatley writes about it.

1772

Sharp helps with James Somerset's case in court. Somerset is freed.

Eighteen men meet with Wheatley to determine she wrote her own poetry.

1773

Wheatley's book is printed in England.

1774

Wheatley writes "Letter to the Rev. Samson Occom."

Equiano asks Granville to help recover a kidnapped friend.

Wheatley is freed from slavery.

1775

Wheatley addresses a poem to George Washington.

1776

July 4th, American leaders sign the Declaration of Independence, creating the United States of America.

1778

Wheatley marries John Peters. All three of their children die as infants.

1780

Wilberforce wins a seat in British Parliament.

1783

Sharp hears about the Zong massacre case from Equiano.

1784

Wheatley dies at the age of thirty-one.

Wilberforce comes to a saving faith in Jesus and meets with John Newton.

Macaulay sails for Jamaica to work a plantation.

1785

Clarkson publishes his prize-winning antislavery essay and becomes an abolitionist.

1787

Clarkson asks Wilberforce to fight for abolition. Wilberforce commits to help enslaved people.

Equiano, with the Sons of Africa group, begins writing anti-slavery letters to newspapers.

1788

Clarkson interviews 20,000 sailors across Britain to show the realities of the slave trade.

1789

Equiano publishes his narrative. He leaves on a book tour through England and meets his wife Susannah.

Macaulay sails home from Jamaica and is saved in Jesus.

Hannah More writes the poem "Slavery."

Wilberforce gives his first speech against the slave trade to Parliament.

Clarkson travels to Paris to try to convince the French to abolish slavery.

1790-1840

The Second Great Awakening focuses on social reform for Christians.

1791-1799

Macaulay serves in Sierra Leone, becoming the governor.

1791

Wilberforce's second motion against slavery has 400,000 signatures.

1792

Sugar is boycotted in Britain.

Equiano marries Susannah. They have two daughters.

1796

Clarkson marries Catherine and have one son.

1797

Sojourner Truth is born between 1797 and 1800.

Equiano dies around age fifty-five.

Wilberforce marries Barbara. They have six children.

1799

Macaulay testifies about the slave trade before Parliament.

Macaulay marries Selina Mills. They have nine children together.

1803

William Knibb is born in England.

1804

Parliament requests new evidence on the slave trade.

1806

Clarkson travels across Britain again to gather new evidence to abolish the slave trade. Nine-year-old Truth is sold at auction.

1807

Wilberforce writes "Letter on the Abolition of the Slave Trade."

The slave trade is abolished in both Britain and America.

1813

Sharp dies.

1817

Frederick Douglass is born, enslaved in Maryland.

1820

Harriet Tubman is born, enslaved in Maryland.

1823

The Clapham Sect forms the Anti-Slavery Society.

1824

Knibb marries Mary. Three of ten children live to adulthood.

Knibb goes to Jamaica teaching 200 children each week and pastoring 500 people.

Douglass is sent to Baltimore to care for a child named Thomas.

1825

Macaulay begins the Anti-Slavery Reporter and serves as the editor for five years.

1826

Truth flees slavery with her youngest daughter.

1828

Truth goes to court to recover her five-year-old son. She is the first black woman to win a case against a white man.

1831-1832

The Jamaican Baptist War begins with a deacon at Knibb's church, involving nearly 60,000 slaves.

1832

Knibb tours Britain, speaking to over 200,000 people about the horrors of slavery.

1833

The Abolition of Slavery Act passes in Britain.

Wilberforce dies three days after witnessing the emancipation of British slaves.

1838

Macaulay dies.

Douglass escapes slavery. He marries Anna and they have five children.

1838-1845

Twenty-two thousand former Jamaican slaves are baptized as new Christians. Knibb baptizes at least 6,000 people.

1840

Clarkson gives the keynote address at the first World Antislavery Convention in London.

1841

Douglass shares his story at an abolitionist convention, beginning his speaking career.

1844

Truth gives her first abolition speech.

1845

Knibb dies of fever.

Douglass publishes his narrative. Douglass speaks against slavery through England and Scotland for a year and a half.

1846

Clarkson dies.

1847

Douglass begins another U.S. speaking tour. He starts publishing the newspaper *North Star*.

1849

Tubman escapes slavery at age twenty-eight.

1850

Truth publishes her narrative.

The Fugitive Slave Law is enacted in the United States.

1851

Truth lectures through New York state. She gives her famous "Ain't I a Woman?" speech.

Tubman makes her first of thirteen journies as a conductor on the Underground Railroad. She rescues around seventy people.

1852

Douglass gives his famous Fourth of July speech.

1861-1865

The American Civil War. The war ends with the emancipation of four million American slaves. Six hundred thousand people die.

Tubman serves as a Union Army spy and nurse, rescuing some 800 liberated slaves in 1863.

1864

Truth works to help black refugees during the Civil War. She meets President Abraham Lincoln.

1869

Tubman marries Nelson Charles Davis and they adopt a little girl. He dies nineteen years later.

Tubman publishes her narrative.

1883

Truth dies.

1884

Douglass marries Helen after the death of Anna.

1890

Tubman has brain surgery to make her skull larger, which helps her condition.

1895

Douglass dies.

1908

Tubman opens the Harriet Tubman Home for the Aged to care for elderly, poor blacks. She is a patient the last two years of her life.

1913

Tubman dies.

WORKS CONSULTED

Bordewich, Fergus M. Bound for Canaan: The Epic Story of the Underground Railroad, America's First Civil Rights Movement. Amistad, 2005.

Bradford, Sarah. Harriet Tubman: The Moses of Her People. Dover Publications, 2004. (Original work published 1869.)

Brain, Jessica. "William Knibb, Abolitionist." Historic UK. https://www.historic-uk.com/HistoryUK/HistoryofBritain/William-Knibb/. Accessed 5/20/22.

Carey, Brycchan. "Granville Sharp (1735-1813)." Brycchan Carey. https://brycchancarey.com/abolition/sharp.htm. Accessed 6/13/2022.

Carey, Brycchan. "Thomas Clarkson (1760-1846)." Brycchan Carey. https://www.brycchancarey.com/abolition/clarkson.htm. Accessed 6/13/2022.

Cook, Faith. Zachary Macaulay. Evangelical Press, 2012.

Douglass, Frederick. Narrative of the Life of Frederick Douglass. Dover Thrift Editions, 1995. (Original work published 1845.)

Drescher, Seymour. Abolition: A History of Slavery and Antislavery. Cambridge University Press, 2009.

Duncan, Dr. Ligon. "Defending the Faith; Denying the Image: 19th Century American Confessional Calvinism in Faithfulness and Failure." Gospel Reformation Network. May 16, 2018. https://gospelreformation.net/defending-the-faith-denying-the-image/. Accessed 9/20/2020.

Duncan, Dr. Ligon. "What About Slavery?" Reformed Theological Seminary. https://rts.edu/resources/what-about-slavery/. Accessed 9/20/2020.

Equiano, Olaudah. The Life of Olaudah Equiano or Gustavus Vassa, The African. Dover Publications, 1999. (Original work published 1789.)

Gates Jr., Henry Louis. The Trials of Phillis Wheatley: America's First Black Poet and Her Encounters with the Founding Fathers. Civitas Books, 2010.

"Granville Sharp." Westminster Abbey. https://www.westminster-abbey.org/abbey-commemorations/commemorations/granville-sharp. Accessed 6/13/2022.

"Granville Sharp (1735-1813)." BBC. https://www.bbc.co.uk/history/historic_figures/sharp_granville.shtml. Accessed 6/13/2022.

Harter, Christopher. "Clarkson, Thomas (1760-1846)." Amistad Research Center. http://amistadresearchcenter.tulane.edu/archon/?p=creators/creator&id=617. Accessed 6/13/2022.

Jackson, Alan. "William Knibb, 1803-1845, Jamaican missionary and slaves' friend." The Victorian Web. https://victorianweb.org/history/knibb/knibb.html. Accessed 5/20/22.

Menikoff, Aaron. "How and Why Did Some Christians Defend Slavery?" The Gospel Coalition. February 24, 2017. https://www.thegospelcoalition.org/article/how-and-why-did-some-christians-defend-slavery/. Accessed 9/20/2020.

Piper, John. Amazing Grace in the Life of William Wilberforce. Crossway, 2007.

Prior, Karen Swallow. Fierce Convictions: The Extraordinary Life of Hannah More—Poet, Reformer, Abolitionist. Nelson Books, 2014, pp. 105-138.

Reese, Ed. Reese Chronological Encyclopedia of Christian Biographies. AMG Publishers, 2007, p. 450.

Scarrott, Diana. "Zachary Macaulay: The statistician who fought to end slavery in British colonies." Royal Statistical Society.

October 4, 2018. https://rss.onlinelibrary.wiley.com/doi/full/10.1111/j.1740-9713.2018.01184.x. Accessed 6/13/2022.

Sharp, Joshua. "Voices: There is no biblical defense for American slavery" Baptist Standard. January 27, 2020. https://www.baptiststandard.com/opinion/voices/no-biblical-defense-american-slavery/. Accessed 9/20/2020.

Sinha, Manisha. The Slave's Cause: A History of Abolition. Yale University Press, 2016.

"Sojourner Truth." Wikipedia. https://en.wikipedia.org/wiki/Sojourner_Truth. Accessed 5/29/2022.

The Great Abolitionists. A. J. Cornell Publications, 2019.

"Thomas Clarkson campaigner for abolition." Revealing Histories Remembering Slavery. http://revealinghistories.org.uk/who-resisted-and-campaigned-for-abolition/people/thomas-clarkson-campaigner-for-abolition.html. Accessed 6/13/2022.

Truth, Sojourner, Olive Gilbert, and Frances W. Titus. Narrative of Sojourner Truth. Musaicum Books, 2017. (Original work published 1850.)

Walsh, Michael, Ed. Dictionary of Christian Biography. The Liturgical Press, 2001, pp. 1108.

Walters, Kerry, Ed. Let Justice Be Done: Writings from American Abolitionists 1688-1865. Orbis Books, 2020.

"William Knibb." Academic Dictionaries and Encyclopedias. https://en-academic.com/dic.nsf/enwiki/4152718. Accessed 5/20/22.

"William Knibb and the "Slave Book"." Brunel University London. January 23, 2020. https://www.brunel.ac.uk/life/library/Archives/News-and-events/News/William-Knibb. Accessed 5/20/2022.

"Zachary Macaulay." Westminster Abbey. https://www.westminster-abbey.org/abbey-commemorations/commemorations/zachary-macaulay. Accessed 6/13/2022.

Danika has done it again! Built on the foundation of God's command to love our neighbors as ourselves, in her Who, What, Why series, Danika comprehensively explores the tragic history of slavery throughout time and throughout the world. It's a sad history, but also a hopeful one, with God's gracious promise ultimately to set captives free.

Douglas Bond
Author of more than thirty books,
including *War in the Wasteland*, and *The Resistance*

I love the effort that Danika Cooley makes in this book to simplify and bring the short stories of several people who fought against slavery and slave trading to the attention of a new generation of young people. We need to know who these real heroes were and especially to know what beliefs made them into champions of this cause. In learning about such men and women, may God make the hearts of our young people today to be brave and so turn them also into world changers for his glory.

Conrad Mbewe
Pastor of Kabwata Baptist Church and founding chancellor
of the African Christian University in Lusaka, Zambia

Danika Cooley had hit the mark with this series. Slavery is an ugly topic, but the stories of the Christian responses to the evil allow hope to shine through. Readers will learn a lot of history, but more importantly they will learn what it means to put the Gospel into action. A series well worth reading.

Linda Finlayson
Author of *God's Timeline* and *God's Bible Timeline*

Other books in the series

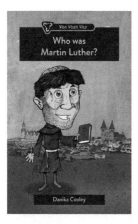

Who was Martin Luther?
Danika Cooley

Martin Luther was a young man who was afraid of a thunderstorm. He was a monk seeking for salvation. He was a reformer who inspired a continent to return to the Word of God. Danika Cooley introduces 9–11 year olds to this key figure in the Reformation.

ISBN: 978-1-5271-0650-5

Why did the Reformation Happen?
Danika Cooley

The Church was following the words of men rather than the Word of God but brave men read God's Word and were saved from their sins. They fought for truth against the most powerful organizations of the time – the Church and the Crown. Danika Cooley explores how God's people changed the Church, Europe and the World.

ISBN: 978-1-5271-0652-9

What was the Gutenberg Bible?
Danika Cooley

Johann Gutenberg invented a world–changing machine that meant people could read God's Word for themselves. The world could share ideas, discoveries and new and God's Word could be quickly, inexpensively and accurately reproduced. Danika Cooley helps 9–11 year-olds discover how the printing press paved the way for the Reformation.

ISBN: 978-1-5271-0651-2

Christian Focus Publications publishes books for adults and children under its four main imprints: Christian Focus, CF4K, Mentor and Christian Heritage. Our books reflect our conviction that God's Word is reliable and Jesus is the way to know him, and live for ever with him.

Our children's publication list covers pre-school to early teens. We also publish personal and family devotional titles, biographies and inspirational stories that children will love.

From pre-school board books to teenage apologetics, we have it covered!

Christian Focus Publications Ltd,
Geanies House, Fearn, Ross-shire,
IV20 1TW, Scotland,
United Kingdom.
www.christianfocus.com